Original title:
Poems from Proxima

Copyright © 2025 Creative Arts Management OÜ
All rights reserved.

Author: Arabella Whitmore
ISBN HARDBACK: 978-1-80567-865-6
ISBN PAPERBACK: 978-1-80567-986-8

Luminous Dreams from Beyond the Veil

In the dark where glowbugs dance,
Aliens plot their next romance.
One brought snacks, the other shoes,
But forgot how to use the snooze.

They giggle under pastel skies,
With bubble tea and festive pies.
They try to hula with delight,
But instead, they just take flight.

The Language of Starlight

Stars gossip in a sparkling blaze,
They trade secrets in wacky ways.
One says 'Earthlings wear such weird hats!'
While another just loves fluffy cats.

They text each other with bright blinks,
Sending emojis and cosmic inks.
A black hole said, 'I'm feeling blue,'
But brightened up when told, 'You too!'

Visions of a Frontier Constellation

Across the void, they take a ride,
On space waves with creatures that glide.
One told jokes about a comet's tail,
That tickled all till they turned pale.

They launched a rocket made of bread,
And giggled hard as it misled.
Bouncing off moons, they lost their way,
But laughed it off—it's just another day!

Chronicles of a Celestial Voyager

On a ship made of sparkles and dreams,
They traveled along authentic streams.
With a coffee pot that brewed stardust,
They found the cosmos a must-visit bust.

They played tag with meteors bright,
Chasing shadows through the galactic night.
One said, 'Watch out, I see a flare!'
But it was just a celestial teddy bear.

Timeless Vistas

A rocket with wheels, oh what a sight,
Zooming through space, day and night.
It stops for a snack at a comet's tail,
And offers its drivers a cosmic trail.

Stars in their pajamas laugh at the chase,
As planets all dance in a whimsical space.
A nebula's wink, a black hole's grin,
In this wild galaxy, everyone wins!

Fusion of the Ethereal

The moon wears a hat made of cheese and jam,
While Martians debate on their favorite spam.
They chat about life in a faraway realm,
And argue which alien's better at helm.

With glasses of juice from a starship's pool,
They craft little gadgets that seem pretty cool.
One floats a balloon shaped like a sun,
While all of their friends just watch and have fun.

When Galaxies Whistle

Oh, the galaxies whistle a fine little tune,
As comets do pirouettes under the moon.
The asteroids jive, in a planetary ball,
And space-time becomes a whimsical hall.

A dance-off breaks out on a ringed old world,
Where aliens twirl and their costumes are swirled.
The laughter is bubbling, the stars all aglow,
When gravity shifts, causing more giggles to flow.

The Silent Symphony of Space

Echoes of laughter, a silent refrain,
As black holes play tag in a cosmic domain.
A supernova bursts, and what a blast it brings,
While aliens gather to crown cosmic kings!

A photon plays drums made of light and of time,
While planets all hum in a celestial rhyme.
The universe chuckles with each little quirk,
Making joy the new law; oh, what a perk!

Reverberations of the Interstellar Passage

In a spaceship made of cheese,
I floated past some cosmic trees.
Space squirrels danced with joyful glee,
Inviting me for a cup of tea.

The Milky Way did twist and twirl,
While Martians tried their best to hurl.
They missed me by a light-year or two,
And laughed so hard, they split a shoe.

A comet came, its tail so bright,
It gave my ship a little fright.
With a wink, it zoomed right by,
Saying, "Catch me if you can, oh my!"

I waved goodbye to the starry crew,
In a game of tag, they all just flew.
And in the end, I found my way,
To the best black hole café in this galaxy array.

A Testament to the Wandering Stars

Stars gathered for a karaoke night,
Singing songs of space with all their might.
A songbird asteroid stole the show,
While Saturn twirled in rings aglow.

Jupiter juggled moons with flair,
As they giggled in the cosmic air.
Uranus rolled with laughter loud,
His gravity too strong for any crowd.

I watched a meteor trip and fall,
A space pirate shouted, "Get up, y'all!"
They dazedly stumbled, laughed and spun,
Claiming the universe was just too fun.

From black holes to novas, all around,
Space humor in every corner found.
With each wonder, I felt so free,
In this stellar circus, just me and the galaxy.

Whispers of Celestial Wanderlust

In the dark, I heard a plea,
A nebula called, come dance with me!
Galaxy giggles echoed and bounced,
As space-time wiggled and announced.

I met a robot with a silly hat,
He said, "I'm from Mars, how 'bout that?"
Together we spun, twirled in flight,
While quasars flickered with delight.

Solar flares played peek-a-boo,
Winking at planets, a lively crew.
Asteroids rolled with comet tails,
Telling tales of intergalactic fails.

As I soared through the cosmic beams,
I couldn't help but laugh at dreams.
With laughter echoing through the stars,
The universe felt like one big bazaar.

Reflections of Uncharted Worlds

In a land where the grass sings loud,
And trees wear hats like a silly crowd,
A purple cow just danced a jig,
While a chicken clucked, feeling big.

The rivers flow with chocolate dreams,
And all around, the sunlight beams,
Fish swim by on bicycles,
Chasing ducks in sparkly spectacles.

Jellybeans rain from the sky,
As birds in tuxedos float on by,
A snail's race is a thrilling sight,
With worms cheering, it's pure delight.

Elder trees with gossip to share,
Whisper tales of who knows where,
A place where alien marbles glow,
And laughing stars dance to and fro.

Whispers of the Cosmic Shore

On the beach of time, seagulls tease,
With surfboards made of grilled cheese,
Crabs wear sunglasses, looking grand,
While jellyfish twirl like a band.

A rocket ship made of candy bars,
Soars past a moon with giant jars,
Filled with giggles and cosmic fun,
Where ticklish comets have to run.

Sandcastles hold big parties here,
With marshmallow fluff and fizzy cheer,
Galactical games of hide and seek,
Where meteors tumble and planets peek.

Curly waves take silly shapes,
As starfish argue about their capes,
Each splash a giggle, each breeze a laugh,
In the cosmic realm, life's a gaff.

Starlit Reveries Beneath Alien Skies

Beneath a sky with polka dots,
Aliens do the tango in quirky spots,
A disco ball hangs from an astroid,
As space cats strut, feeling overjoyed.

Galaxies spin with jelly rolls,
While cosmic ice cream tempts our souls,
Bubblegum planets in every hue,
Launch us into a dance that's new.

While comets race in tandem loops,
Asteroids host space-dancing groups,
A giant worm undulates with style,
Inviting all to join the smile.

As shooting stars write jokes on the air,
And planets giggle without a care,
These starlit dreams, oh what a scene,
In a universe where fun reigns supreme.

Rhapsody in the Galactic Outback

In the outback of space, cows float with glee,
Aliens teach them to dance under the tree.
With twinkling stars, they spark and they spin,
A funky line-dance, let the party begin!

Kangaroos in spacesuits bounce with great style,
Using jetpacks to hop, they go an extra mile.
Martians chuckle as they sip cosmic stew,
While blue space kangaroos sing a tune or two.

Tales of Light in the Void

In the dark, where shadows play peek-a-boo,
A comet zooms past, with a tail made of goo.
Wormholes giggle, swirling round and round,
As twinkling stars slapstick-fall to the ground.

A space octopus juggles black holes with flair,
Telling jokes to the nebulae, just hanging there.
Supernova sneezes, bursts into a fit,
Creating new worlds, oh, what a cosmic skit!

Cosmic Corners of a Timeless World

In corners of cosmos, where giggles abide,
Stars play hide-and-seek, they take it in stride.
A planet named Chuckle swirls in delight,
With laughter so bright, it outshines the night!

Eternal echoes of a cosmic choir,
Singing songs of the galaxies, lifting us higher.
Time-traveling turtles recite funny tales,
While meteors race in mismatched scaled sails.

A Glimpse through Cosmic Gates

Beyond cosmic gates where the funny things dwell,
Jokesters of the universe weave tales to tell.
Celestial clowns ride comets and beams,
Tickling the void, causing space giggle-teams.

In this realm of wonder, the unthinkable thrives,
A sun takes a nap while a rogue moon jives.
Quasars play catch with comets in flight,
Bouncing off stardust, all through the night!

Melodies from an Absent Sun

Balloons float high, made of gas,
As Martians whistle, it's quite the sass.
They dance in circles, wearing hats,
While sipping tea with friendly cats.

They sing of worlds where socks get lost,
And cosmic pies are worth the cost.
A comet swings by, chimes a tune,
And ducks parade beneath the moon.

A planet trips, stumbles in space,
Landing near, with a funny face.
Jovian jesters juggle, quite a sight,
While Saturn rings wink, oh what a night!

In silence, black holes chuckle loud,
At twinkling stars that feel so proud.
With every note in this wild ride,
Galactic giggles, they cannot hide.

The Dance of Celestial Shadows

Shadows pirouette, in cosmic play,
Doing the cha-cha, in a light gray.
Lunar llamas leap and bound,
As meteors jazz across the ground.

A space worm wriggles, doing the twist,
While planets giggle, they can't resist.
Uranus spins with a silly grin,
As comets twirl with a cheeky spin.

Sirens in orbit hum a tune,
While asteroids boogie to the moon.
Stars play tag, dodging black holes,
In the grand ball where laughter rolls.

The starlight winks, oh what a spree,
As the Milky Way serves cosmic tea.
In the dance of shadows, joy unfolds,
Every move told in laughter bold.

Interstellar Letters Untold

A letter floats from Mars to me,
Written in laughter, not in glee.
It scribbles 'Hi!' in extra-large fonts,
And doodles aliens in funny pants.

Venus writes back with a flourish and spin,
'Life here's a blast, let the fun begin!'
She sends cosmic cookies that bounce and sing,
With a side note: 'Earthling, please bring bling!'

Jupiter's note spills coffee with flair,
Saying 'Wish you were here, it's no longer fair!'
He sends a postcard of swirling storms,
While Saturn's rings fashion strange forms.

The galaxy chuckles, each letter a jest,
Sending their love, it's simply the best.
With interstellar jokes, we share and delight,
Laughter echoes through the endless night.

Chasing Radiance in the Dark

In cosmic corners where shadows fester,
Glowworms giggle, a glowing jester.
They peek through voids, like kids at play,
Chasing the light that leads them astray.

Nebulae whisper, with secrets to keep,
While starfish in space have a cosmic leap.
They flip through the stardust, splashing in glee,
Singing, 'Find the glow, won't you join me?'

Darkness chuckles as comets race,
Fumbling for light in this grand, vast space.
With every blip and blink they chase,
Radiance flickers, a dance, a grace.

In the backdrop of black, we laugh and spin,
As the universe teases, inviting us in.
Chasing the spark in dimness so stark,
Joy floats in quarks, igniting the dark.

Lament of an Abandoned World

Once a vibrant place to play,
Now a dusty, quiet sway.
Aliens took my favorite toy,
Leaving me a space-age decoy.

Rover dogs chase shooting stars,
While I ponder life on Mars.
What happened to the lively fun?
Now it's all just cosmic run.

Galactic parties filled the skies,
Now it's just a sad disguise.
I send a note on comet's tail,
To find some pals within the pale.

Oh universe, you seem so vast,
Where's the humor from the past?
With giggles lost in swirling void,
I'm left here just a little annoyed.

Voyages through Cosmic Mysteries

On a ship made of tinfoil bright,
I sail through stars, what a sight!
With space snacks packed in a tray,
    Galactic travel's here to stay!

I met a dwarf who told me jokes,
While dodging rocks and flocks of stokes.
His punchlines flew like shooting stars,
    We laughed till we hit Mars.

Planets dance a merry jig,
My spaceship boogies, oh so big!
With every twist and cosmic turn,
I learn new tricks on how to churn.

Navigating through stardust trails,
    Life's a joke with no entails.
So grab a friend and float away,
In quirky realms where we can play.

Threads of Light in the Darkness

In shadows deep, I weave my dreams,
With cosmic yarn and glitter beams.
I knit a nebula, nice and bright,
While crafting stars with all my might.

A comet's tail, a flashing glow,
Is just the start of my grand show.
I wrap the moons in laughter's thread,
Creating smiles across the spread.

But in this space of fluffy fun,
My knitting needles come undone!
A cosmic knot, a tangled plight,
Yet still I twinkle, full of light.

So here I sit among the gloom,
With shining threads, I banish doom.
This fabric of the universe,
Is stitched with giggles, not a curse!

Pulsars and Dreams of Other Realms

Bright pulsars beep a silly tune,
Dancing to the cosmic moon.
I close my eyes and drift away,
To lands where aliens love to play.

With every pulse, a funny tale,
Of quirky critters that prevail.
They wear big hats and silly shoes,
In colors no one dares to choose.

In dreams, I bounce from star to star,
Sharing jokes with friends afar.
We trade our laughs like cosmic goods,
In joy-filled interstellar hoods.

So, let the pulsars lead the way,
To realms where fun is here to stay.
And with each pulse, remember this:
The universe is built on bliss!

Exoplanetary Dreams and Stellar Realities

In dreams I sail on comet tails,
Wearing socks with silly scales.
Laughter echoes past the stars,
Chasing space ducks and candy bars.

Glowing moons, they wink and tease,
Making mischief with cosmic breeze.
Gravity silly, I float in glee,
Like an astronaut sipping sweet tea.

The sun is a giant disco ball,
Where aliens dance, oh what a haul!
They invite me to join the fun,
On a space trip, oh what a run!

In wild dreams, the galaxies spin,
As I wear a hat that's shaped like sin.
Reality beckons, but I ignore,
In my world, there's always more.

The Symphony of Celestial Travelers

A band of stars with twinkling eyes,
Play cosmic tunes beneath night skies.
A supernova on the drum set,
Giving rhythm to the space duet.

Aliens waltz with comets bright,
Dancing with glee in the pale starlight.
Mars strums softly on Moon's lute,
While Saturn spins in a glittery suit.

Galactic melodies fill the void,
Laughing at rules they've all destroyed.
A chorus of planets sings along,
In this universe where we belong.

With every note, new dreams ignite,
As laughter echoes through the night.
In this orchestra of the bizarre,
We jam along, and ride each star.

Stories Beneath a Foreign Sky

Under a sky not of our hue,
I found a tree that grew stew.
Its branches danced with shimm'ring light,
While squirrels rode rockets, what a sight!

One whispered tales from Venus's shore,
Of chocolate rain and so much more.
With every word, my laughter soared,
As the stars and I struck up a chord.

Space creatures chewed on candy beams,
And shared wild tales of their red dreams.
A nebula swirled with giggles bright,
As we mapped out the comical night.

The moon offered pie, sweet and round,
With jellied planets all around.
The stars scribbled down our fun spree,
In stories shared amongst the free.

Ballet of the Birthright Stars

In pirouettes of shimmering glow,
Stars twirl and leap in a cosmic show.
The Milky Way's a stage so wide,
Where meteors glide with comical pride.

Dressed in dust from head to toe,
These planets dance to a jazzy flow.
They trip on stardust, giggle, and spin,
In a ballet where chaos wears a grin.

Supernovae leap in grand display,
As black holes swirl with a dash of play.
Lunar lights cha-cha across dark space,
Creating laughter in the twinkling place.

Our universe bursts with laughter loud,
Where each star curtsies, feeling proud.
For in this ballet of fiery zest,
Every twinkle is a prank at best.

Fragments of Cosmic Whimsy

In the void where comets play,
A dancing quasar strays,
Twirling like it's on a spree,
Bumping into asteroids with glee.

Stars in pajamas, shining bright,
Having pillow fights at night,
Coffee break on Saturn's rings,
Laughing at the silliest things.

Nebulae wear funny hats,
Making faces like old cats,
Gravitational pulls with flair,
Who knew space could be so rare?

Galaxies spin with wicked zest,
Starry laughs, the universal jest,
In this vast and twinkling stage,
Cosmic humor on every page.

Cries of a Dying Star

Once a giant, now a spark,
Screaming out in cosmic park,
'Will I fade or just explode?'
Pondering on this heavy load.

Wishing for some stellar cheer,
A supernova's messy smear,
Friends are drifting, lost in space,
Hearts afloat, at an odd pace.

To black hole or not to go,
A dilemma with cosmic flow,
Ripping fabric, such a fuss,
Still humor finds a way to trust.

'Hey there, planet, drop a snack!'
In this void, we'll all just crack,
As I twinkle, dim my light,
Remember me, oh, what a sight!

Navigating the Celestial Labyrinth

Galactic highways twist and turn,
Stars with maps, and yet they burn,
'Which way to the cosmic fair?'
'Oh dear, we're lost, beyond despair!'

Planets chuckle, taking bets,
'Bet the Martians get upset!'
With every wrong way that they steer,
'We'll find a taco stand, I fear!'

Comets pass with winks and smiles,
While black holes pull with tricky styles,
Constellations argue which is best,
'Forget it, let's just take a rest!'

Through wormholes and the cosmic sea,
Navigating absurdity,
At every turn, a giggle waits,
As laughter echoes through the gates.

Twilight of the Alien Garden

In the twilight, flowers beam,
Purple laughter in moonlit gleam,
Strange fruits dance with wobbly grace,
Tickling leaves, a cheeky chase.

Gnomes with antennas cultivate,
Berries that giggle, growing great,
Photosynthesis turned to dance,
Each bloom bearing a silly chance.

Solar rays play hide and seek,
While veggies plot a sneak peek,
'Let's hold hands and make some noise!'
In this garden, fun's the choice!

As stars wink down with a grin,
The aliens all join in the spin,
Underneath this vibrant sky,
Twilight whispers, 'Let's all fly!'

Beneath the Glimmering Expanse

Aliens gather for a dance,
Wobbling weird in their bright pants.
They sip on fizzy moonlight drinks,
And sing of things that make us think.

One says Earth's humor's quite absurd,
They laugh at jokes we've never heard.
A comet plays the ukulele,
As Martian chefs fry space chili!

Jupiter's clouds can't hold the beat,
While Saturn's rings twirl on their feet.
They joke 'bout gravity's bad breath,
And share their tales of silly death.

So next time you gaze at the sky,
Remember laughter's floating by.
Those twinkling lights in the dark place,
Might just be aliens' party space!

Lost in Cosmic Translation

A message comes from far away,
It's filled with words we can't relay.
We send back jokes of socks and fries,
But they reply with puzzled sighs.

A probe is sent to bridge the gap,
And finds a squid in a top hat.
It speaks in rhymes, dances on walls,
But ends up just confusing us all.

As numbers spin in dizzying loops,
We mix our snacks with alien soups.
The translation fails, but no one cares,
We share our laughs and odd stares.

So here's to language, lost at sea,
In cosmic chatter, wild and free.
From Earth to stars, we send our cheer,
Hoping the jokes are loud and clear!

Stardust and Secrets

Stardust sprinkled on my head,
Turns my cereal into spread!
I eat my breakfast in a trance,
While meteors around me dance.

A galaxy spins with a big cheer,
"Earthlings, try our cosmic beer!"
It tastes like berries, sweet and bright,
And gives me dreams of silly flight.

The moon whispers tales of lost socks,
Where all the creatures play with clocks.
They tick and tock without a care,
In a universe of joyful flare.

Under a sky of swirling fun,
I realize I am not the only one.
Secrets hide in shining dust,
Laughter glows in the cosmic rust!

Chronicles of the Unseen

In a nebula, strange things abound,
Invisible critters flit around.
They play hide and seek with our minds,
Lighting up stars of different kinds.

One whispers tales of galactic pies,
While another shows off their new ties.
Did you know black holes are fun to play?
They stretch and bend in a wacky way!

They laugh at humans and their fears,
And toast to laughter across the years.
With a wink, they slip into the night,
Leaving us wondering what was right.

So raise a glass to all the tricks,
Of unseen friends with cosmic flicks.
In every shadow, joy might be,
Hidden in laughs of the galaxy!

Glamor of the Forgotten Cosmos

In a galaxy, lost and wide,
There danced two moons, side by side.
With shoes made of stardust, they twirled,
In a plot so strange, it unfurled.

Comets laughed as they zoomed by,
Shooting sparks, oh my, oh my!
Black holes chuckled, making a fuss,
While planets debated, what's all this?

Asteroids joined with a clatter,
Bumping and bouncing, what's the matter?
They wore funny hats made of ice,
And claimed that was their only vice.

So raise a toast to space's play,
Where glittering trails lead the way.
In this forgotten cosmic show,
Even stars can be quite the clown, you know!

Waiting for a Star to Speak

A star sat quietly, full of hope,
Wishing to chat, learn how to cope.
With a twinkle and a giggle, it sighed,
Yet no one knew what it had inside.

Comets zipped past, full of cheer,
Said, 'Just shout out, we're always near!'
But the star thought it best to be shy,
So it blinked once and said, 'Why try?'

The universe watched with bated breath,
For the day it would share its depth.
But in silence, it winked, still alone,
Creating a spectacle all its own.

At last it bellowed, 'Hello, my dear!'
But only silence drew near.
Now it's the funniest star in the sky,
Waiting for someone to give it a try!

Elysium on the Fringes of Space

At the edge of nothing, where dreams collide,
Lived a squad of stars, oh what a ride!
They threw a party with moonbeam snacks,
And invited the comets, with plenty of lacks.

The nebula joined with colors so bold,
Dancing in hues, brilliant and gold.
While black holes served coffee, swirling and strong,
Saying, 'One sip and you'll dance all night long!'

Laughter erupted; it echoed through time,
Space was alive with laughter and rhyme.
The planets spun jokes, oh what a sight,
In this fringe Elysium, hearts took flight.

So join the fest with a wink and a grin,
Where dark matter gives everyone a spin.
You might just find in this cosmic embrace,
Even the mundane finds a funny place!

Memories of an Astral Nomad

An astral nomad rolled on a ball,
Chasing the echoes of a starry call.
With sandals of stardust and trails of light,
He traveled the cosmos, both day and night.

He'd stop to chat with a passing star,
Swap tales of travels near and far.
"Oh, do tell me your silliest blunder,
Most stars never make it past the thunder!"

With comets as friends, they played a game,
Of tag in the silence, it wasn't the same.
The nomad laughed, while twirling around,
Making memories in the vast, cosmic sound.

As he wandered through depths of the sky,
He gathered his giggles, oh how they fly!
For in this vast and starry realm,
A humor so bright is at the helm!

Echoes of an Alien Dream

In the night, a Martian danced,
With three legs and a funny glance.
He tripped on his own green feet,
Made a joke, then fell on his seat.

Zebras in space wear polka dots,
Telling tales of silly robots.
They sip on cosmic lemonade,
And laugh at gravity's escapade.

A comet whizzed by, what a sight,
Fell right into a UFO's flight.
The aliens cheered, a galactic feast,
With moon cheese burgers, to say the least!

So, when you gaze at stars up high,
Remember this: they laugh and fly.
In the cosmos, joy reigns supreme,
Echoes of an alien dream.

Starlit Conversations

Stars gossip in twinkling tones,
While comets play hopscotch with drones.
One star said, 'I'm feeling round,'
The other laughed, 'You're space-bound!'

Galactic critters tell tall tales,
Of cosmic trains with rainbow trails.
They chat about their traveling woes,
And the best snacks from black hole shows.

Planetary parties bring quite the scene,
With dancing rings and a glowing sheen.
Aliens boast, 'Our moves are slick!'
While Jupiter's storms just tap dance quick.

In starlit nights, laughter is gold,
With secrets of the universe told.
Join the chatter, so free and bright,
Where every joke shines in the night.

The Language of the Nebula

Fluffy clouds in vibrant hues,
Whisper jokes, just like a muse.
'What's a star's favorite snack?' they chime,
'Galactic chips, they're simply prime!'

Nebulae giggle, they twist and twirl,
Sharing secrets with the whirl.
A comet shouted, 'I'm faster than light!'
A quasar winked, 'In games, I'm a fright!'

Gravity's pull can't hold them down,
As they spin around in a cosmic gown.
Their language flows like floating dust,
In laughter and joy, we all must trust.

Through stardust trails, their voices ring,
A melody of fun they sing.
The universe knows, it's plain to see,
Laughter connects you and me.

Astral Reveries

Dreamers float on silver streams,
With quirky thoughts and wild dreams.
A space cat wearing a tin foil hat,
Snores softly, imagine that!

Shooting stars take a dive,
Wishing to win the galactic jive.
They spin and twirl, a dazzling sight,
As aliens applaud their light-filled flight.

Moonbeams giggle in the dark,
While playful meteors leave a spark.
They banter about who's fast and slow,
In a cosmic race through stars aglow.

In astral lands where wackiness reigns,
With laughter echoing in celestial veins.
Embrace the whimsy, let spirits soar,
In the universe's heart, forevermore.

In the Orbit of Imagination

In a rocket made of cheese,
We'd dance with witty mice,
With moonbeam hats and shimmering capes,
Oh, what a silly paradise.

Our comet tails are sparkling bright,
As we twirl in goofy glee,
Jupiter's got the best dance floor,
And Saturn joins in our spree.

The stars are bursting out in laughs,
As we juggle solar flares,
With each silly cosmic giggle,
We banish all our cares.

In our galaxy of dreams,
We'll ride on laughter's flight,
Who knew the cosmos could be so fun,
With humor shining bright!

Celestial Murmurs

The moon whispers jokes so sweet,
But they're old as ancient dust,
"Why did Mars cross the Milky Way?
To prove he was a must!"

Stars giggle in a twinkling way,
As galaxies start to tease,
"Hey Earth! You're spinning like a top,
Do you ever get dizzy knees?"

On asteroids, we'll hold a show,
With comets as our fans,
We'll share our funny little tales,
And hold out funny hands.

Through cosmic winds, the laughter flies,
As we float on stardust trails,
Who knew the universe had jokes,
With punchlines tied with sails?

Celestial Cartography

Sketching maps with cosmic crayons,
Drawing planets with a grin,
"Oops! Is that a doodle of Pluto,
Or just some pizza spin?"

Navigating through a starry maze,
With laughter as our guide,
"Take a left at the laughing star,
And go where the giggles reside."

Our chart of jokes and silly sights,
Is filled with marshmallow moons,
As we plot a course through humor,
To disco on late afternoons.

Galactic maps of chuckling light,
Unfolding joy with every click,
In this interstellar doodle land,
Not one will find a trick!

Beyond the Solar Veil

Past the sunlit veil of play,
Where laughter blooms like stars,
We'll tickle comets, race with glee,
Defying all the cosmic bars.

In the shaded spots of night,
We'll tell tales of cosmic fools,
With aliens in silly hats,
And gravity-defying stools.

Dancing on the rings of fate,
We'll trip in zero-G,
With every bounce and funny fall,
We'll burst with joy, you'll see!

So join us in this merry chase,
Where galaxies twirl and sway,
In the fun beyond the solar veil,
We'll giggle night and day!

Celestial Boundaries and Fading Echoes

Beyond the stars, we dare to pry,
Aliens giggle as they float by.
With spaghetti legs and jelly beams,
We'll outdance them in our wild dreams.

Galactic pigeons dropping stars,
They race us round through cosmic bars.
We sip from nebulae, floating high,
With comets whizzing, just to try.

When Jupiter winks with a cheeky grin,
We toss our hats and spin to win.
Asteroids rolling, making a mess,
Is that a dance? Or just pure stress?

So we float on, with laughter loud,
In the vacuum, we feel so proud.
With hiccuping planets in the night,
Who knew space would feel so light?

Songs for the Celestial Driftwood

Driftwood hails from waves that sing,
Floating stars might sprout some wings.
With a wink, they twirl and sway,
To cosmic tunes, they seize the day.

Bubbles burst like laughter's flight,
Dancing shadows in the night.
A sunbeam's giggle, what a sight,
Making waves with pure delight.

Asteroids wearing goofy hats,
Glare at space whales and their chats.
We groove aboard our wooden raft,
With merry tunes and playful craft.

Let's whistle melodies with the breeze,
As every galaxy aims to tease.
In this vastness, jokes abound,
Drifting ever, singing round and round.

Horizons of an Enigmatic Twilight

At twilight's edge, the shadows play,
With giggling moons that lead astray.
Stars do the tango with a bounce,
Unruly comets in a pounce.

Planets gossip with cheeky flair,
Swapping secrets in cosmic air.
Twinkling lights with a wink and nod,
What's next? A dance-off, oh my God!

With paintbrush suns and brushstroke skies,
Planets burst forth with playful sighs.
Gravity's pulling our silly feet,
As we skip through space, oh what a feat!

Beware the black hole's hungry grin,
It might just swallow your best friend's kin.
But here we laugh, on this wild ride,
With golden dreams twinkling wide.

From the Heart of a Distant Cosmos

From realms afar, our phones do ring,
Aliens asking, 'Can you sing?'
With echoes soft as whispers fade,
We giggle at all the jokes they've made.

Nebulae wrap us in patches bright,
Questioning if dancing feels right.
Stars roll their eyes, they've seen it all,
Yet here we bounce, we'll never fall.

The vacuum of space tries to hold tight,
But laughter bursts, igniting the night.
We play tag with meteors, oh so spry,
Who knew distances could make us fly?

So here's to laughter in all the skies,
Where humor lifts us, and spirit flies.
Each distant world, with its own delight,
Nods along in our joyful flight.

Whispers of the Binary Stars

Two stars were seen having a chat,
One said, "How's your orbit, you fat?"
The other replied with a twinkling grin,
"Just trying to lose weight, it's a stellar sin!"

They giggled and giggled, their light set to dance,
While meteors blushed at their cosmic romance.
"You're my twin flame," one star started to croon,
"But last time you shone, I thought it was noon!"

Black holes made jokes about space-time woes,
While asteroids laughed, striking silly poses.
In the void of the dark, there's a joy to be found,
Being silly in space is the best kind of sound!

So cheers to the stars with their comical flair,
In this vast universe, let's lighten the air.
Here's to laughter that glows like a supernova's glow,
For out here in cosmos, it's all just a show!

Celestial Echoes

In the quiet of space, hear the echoing fun,
Where comets make jokes faster than light can run.
"Why did the nebula bring a towel?" said one,
"Because it's always wet in the cosmic pun!"

Planets were rolling, like kids on the grass,
While Saturn's rings were just glittery sass.
"I'm the best dress, don't you think, oh dear?"
"You've got more bling than a planet in gear!"

Meteors burst out with their popping laughs,
Crashing through silence, they're brilliant gaffes.
"Gravity's a joke, it pulls us so tight,"
"But I love that it makes us dance through the night!"

So raise up your glass to the quirks of our sky,
To laughter and whimsy that will never die.
For in this grand dance of the stellar parade,
We find that our joy in the cosmos won't fade!

Journey to the Distant Light

Blast off, dear friend, it's a cosmic spree,
With rockets that giggle, how wild can we be?
"To the distant light!" shouted one with a grin,
"I hope we don't meet any martians with skin!"

The spaceship wobbled, as laughter took flight,
And aliens peeked out, a delightful sight.
"Hey, Earthlings, come play! We've got snacks and games!"
"Just don't bring the probes, they're the ones with the names!"

Through asteroid fields, they played tag and hide,
Of course, a few comets just couldn't abide.
"Let's race to the nebula and see who is fast!"
"But don't lose your heads, or your jokes won't last!"

So spinning through space, what a marvelous ride,
With friends from afar, and nowhere to hide.
In this journey of laughter among the great stars,
Every giggle and chuckle is truly ours!

Shadows on the Cosmic Shore

Footprints in stardust, what a silly place,
Waves of the cosmos, gotta keep up the pace.
"Watch out for aliens!" someone shouted in fright,
But it turned out they just wanted to dance in the light!

Saturn trod softly, with rings that would sway,
While Jupiter juggled, in its mighty way.
"Are you going to the moon for a picnic?" they yelled,
"To snack on some craters, where dreams are upheld!"

The sun cast a shadow that twisted and spun,
Making patterns of giggles, oh what fun!
Stars sang in harmony, a jolly refrain,
While black holes just chuckled at our silly gain!

So here on this shore, where the quirks come alive,
We'll laugh with the cosmos, where wonders arrive.
In the shadows of space, let's dance like we're bold,
For laughter is timeless, and never grows old!

Secrets in the Nebula's Embrace

In the mist where stars giggle,
Aliens dance with a wiggle.
They share jokes with asteroids bright,
As comets swerve left and right.

The planets chuckle, their rings spin,
While moons play hide and seek, with a grin.
UFOs zap by, yelling, "Surprise!"
Their laughter echoes through the skies.

A stardust cat, with a sneeze,
Makes a black hole, if you please.
And meteors toss candy like snow,
As interstellar parties steal the show.

In this space where silliness swells,
Galactic mischief and giggles dwell.
So, strap in tight for a raucous ride,
Amongst the stars, where mirth won't hide.

Harmonies from the Galactic Outlands

In the void, a banjo strums,
While a comet hums, oh, so fun!
Pulsars tap their shiny feet,
As quasars groove to an inky beat.

The moons serenade with soft coos,
Jupiter's storms yell, "We love blues!"
Sing along with the cosmic crew,
As Saturn's rings twirl, it's true!

Asteroids clink like chilled glass,
While nebulae swirl with sass.
Clusters of stars join the song,
As they shine bright and bop along.

Through the outlands, laughter rings,
Even the black holes pull funny strings.
So come one, come all, let's join the jam,
In this universe, you're the star, blam!

Reflections in the Abyss of Space

In the darkness where giggles reside,
A space pirate with nowhere to hide.
He chuckles at shadows, gives a wink,
As asteroids whisper secrets of ink.

The void plays tricks, a game of peek,
With planets that pop out, squeaking, "Geek!"
A black hole swallows laughter whole,
Then spits it back, personalized, role.

Supernovae burst with a puff,
Filling the night with a sparkle, so tough.
While aliens juggling flaming stars,
Yell, "Catch this!" as they fly through bars.

In this abyss, where silliness reigns,
The universe gives us humorous gains.
So grin wide, let your spirits soar,
In the deep, where fun is never a bore.

Tides of Time from the Beyond

Time waves roll like a cosmic tide,
Galaxies surf, they take a ride.
Gravity's game of tug-and-pull,
Has quarks giggling, 'It's wonderful!'

Through wormholes, laughter flows,
Backwards and forwards, it ebbs and grows.
With every tick, a joke is made,
Futures chuckle in a light parade.

Silly clocks march with ridiculous glee,
Ticking to rhythms of a cosmic spree.
As starry sand drips in a whimsical hourglass,
They whisper jokes that spark and sizzle fast.

So ride the waves of infinite jest,
In the beyond, where whimsy is best.
For in the tides of time's embrace,
There's always room for a merry face.

Woven Threads of Galactic Time

In a fabric of stars, they weave with glee,
Alien squirrels throw cosmic confetti.
Planets spin wildly, a dance of the night,
While comets play tag in the shimmering light.

Every tick of a clock, a giggle goes by,
With time-traveling spoons that can suddenly fly.
A calendar flips, and it's disco again,
As black holes burst forth with a chorus of 'When?'

They stitch up the universe, thread by thread,
With pasta of stardust, oh, who needs good bread?
Knitting affects on a galactic scale,
As kittens on Mars plan an interstellar sail.

Each moment's a noodle, twisty and free,
Wrapped in the laughter of moments we see.
So let's bow to the cosmos, our whimsical yarn,
As we dance on planets with freedom to charm.

The Spirit of Unseen Sanctuaries

In the hush of the night, under mystical skies,
Ghosts of the aliens plot their next surprise.
They slip through the shadows, all stealthy and spry,
With umbrellas of stardust that twinkle and fly.

Whispers of spirits sweetly convene,
Holding galactic feasts that are fit for a queen.
Antigravity cakes and drinks made of light,
Feed a legion of wizards who dance out of sight.

A party of brooms and quirky abodes,
Where walls clap along to an unearthly code.
Juggling black holes, they laugh with delight,
Underneath a moon that's a giant disco light.

So toast to the shadows, the unseen the bright,
In sanctuaries hidden, a wondrous delight.
For if you believe, with a grin and a cheer,
You might catch a glimpse of what's happening here.

Eclipsed Echoes of Distant Lives

In faraway valleys where echoes reside,
Funny old aliens begin to collide.
Their laughter like music, a festival's beat,
As they juggle the stars and all that's discreet.

An eclipse comes to play, wearing shades with flair,
A cosmic production with actors to spare.
They trip on their comets, in laughter, they swerve,
Performing grand slides on a lunar curve.

Each whisper a giggle from ages gone by,
As echoes respond to the sounds of the sky.
What secrets they hold in the pulse of the night,
Like bananas that dance when you switch on the light.

So let's swirl in the chaos of moments so rare,
And toast to the echoes, the giggles we share.
For in every dark shadow, funny lives shine,
In the dance of the cosmos, our spirits entwine.

Stargazer's Soliloquy

A stargazer sat with a telescope wide,
He wondered if aliens were taking a ride.
With marshmallow ships and cotton candy sails,
A whimsical crew that regales with tales.

He peered through the lens, his eyes bulged with glee,
Expecting to see little folks sipping tea.
But all he found was a galactic parade,
Of wiggly creatures that danced in the shade.

"Come, join us!" they beckoned, with giggles all bright,
"We're hosting a feast for the stars tonight!"
So he tossed aside caution, leaped right through the feel,
To dance with the cosmos, and let fate reveal.

In encounters of laughter, in moments of fun,
The stargazer twirled with the moon and the sun.
So when you look up, heed the giggle's sweet rush,
For behind every star, there's a stellar hush.

Embracing the Orbit of Dreams

In a galaxy where sneakers glow,
Stars trade secrets with a goofy crow.
Asteroids waltz, in their fancy shoes,
As meteors giggle, spreading their blues.

Planets play tag, spinning with glee,
While comets do donuts, just wait and see.
Black holes are crevices for hide and seek,
Where the bravest of stardust dare-to-squeak.

Fragments of a Cosmic Diary

Yesterday's sun had a ticklish flare,
It sneezed out solar winds, sent dust everywhere.
Jupiter's moons throw a crazy bash,
With pizza and punch, they gather in a flash.

Venus tried to dance but tripped on her light,
And Mars brought confetti, it was quite the sight.
Mercury laughed till his orbit ached,
Saying 'Next time, more snacks! That's just what I make!'

Celestial Cartography of Forgotten Stars

Galaxies draw maps on the backs of a mote,
While quasars sip juice from a drifting boat.
Nebulas giggle as they fluff up their fluff,
Winding around comets, just catching the stuff.

Eclipses play peek-a-boo, such naughty fun,
As sunbeams high-five, like rays on the run.
Constellations argue over who's the best,
While stardust spreads secrets, a glittering jest.

Glimpses of the Infinite Playground

In the cosmic sandbox, swings made of light,
Hold giggling star-kids playing all night.
Supernovas bounce like they're on a spree,
While gravity tickles, making all giggle with glee.

Meteor slides whoosh with gleaming trails,
Saturn takes selfies, with his festive veils.
In this wild circus, laughter's the key,
As space fills with joy, like a cosmic jubilee.

Vibrations from the Celestial Sea

In the ether, fish take flight,
Juggling stars, they glow so bright.
With every splash, they twirl and spin,
I dropped my lunch—what a cosmic win!

Galloping comets join the race,
Chasing tails in endless space.
One tripped over a wandering moon,
'Oops!' it cried, 'I'll be home by noon!'

Riding waves of giggles loud,
Saturn's rings, a laughter crowd.
They threw a party, no one knew,
Except the asteroids; they brought the brew!

Under the light of a winking star,
We danced with glee, just near and far.
The universe chuckled, what a sight,
In this cosmic jest, we felt so light!

Nightfall on the Outer Rim

When twilight whispers, wink and nod,
Aliens ply their interstellar fraud.
The moon just giggled, holding her sides,
Watching Martians paint their rides.

Stars lined up for a midnight show,
One wore a hat, a dazzling bow.
They tripped and fumbled on the beam,
Even the black holes joined the theme!

A comet strummed its tail like a guitar,
Singing songs that traveled far.
They cracked jokes that made meteors cry,
"Oh please, don't toss me out of the sky!"

In the shadows, a space cat yawned,
Flicked a tail, where has my snack spawned?
Chasing photons, mighty and sly,
"Just a nibble," it said, "don't be shy!"

Emissaries from the Starry Expanse

From beyond, they came, a quirky crew,
Unraveled tinfoil, and they knew what to do.
With straws in hand, they sipped sweet light,
"Is this what they meant by 'cosmic delight'?"

They brought their gadgets, what a sight,
Clipped off their wings, to run in flight.
One spilled juice on a solar flare,
"Oops, that's hot, but I don't care!"

They played hopscotch on stardust trails,
Giggling loudly, telling tall tales.
But fell on asteroids—what a mess,
"Next time, let's try less finesse!"

A round of laughs echoed through space,
As they bounced along in a cheeky race.
With every twinkle, they were grinning wide,
Waving their flags of galactic pride!

Whispers of Cosmic Histories

In the silence, secrets hum,
Galaxies gossip, oh so fun!
"Did you hear what happened to Mars?
He tried to dance with Venus at the bars!"

Comets tell tales, ancient lore,
While waiters on moons offer snacks galore.
Black holes chuckle, as they feast,
On stardust muffins, feeling at least!

All planets gather for a chat,
Swapping gossip like, 'What's up with that?'
Planets collide with laughter absurd,
"We should market this, it's the best heard!"

From the quiet depths to the edge of night,
Cosmic humor shines oh so bright.
In the universe's grand giggle fest,
I'll toast my stars, they are simply the best!

Stardust Scribbles

In cosmic cafes, stars spill their tea,
Planets giggle, as they spin with glee.
A comet trips, it leaps and it bounds,
Sending shockwaves, oh what silly sounds!

Nebulae laugh, with colors so bright,
Drawing doodles in the vast, endless night.
Black holes chuckle, they're quite a delight,
Swallowing secrets, gone out of sight!

Asteroids dance in a wobbly row,
Bumping through space, with no sense of flow.
They form a conga to a cosmic tune,
Making moons giggle, under the moon!

Near a supernova, a fun party's planned,
With space dust flying, oh isn't it grand?
Galactic jokers share laughter and fun,
In this quirky realm, where joy's never done!

Echoes from Beyond the Event Horizon

Whispers of light from a black hole abyss,
Are just giggles that space cannot miss.
Stars huddle close, in a game of peek,
While photons dash, they play hide and seek!

Gravity's pull makes the wise ones sway,
As silly space travelers giggle and play.
A neutron star hums a jovial tune,
While quarks do the tango, 'neath a laughing moon!

Time bends and warps, laughs echo in space,
As comets zip by with astonishing grace.
From faraway realms, we hear all the fun,
Science and laughter, together as one!

Falling through time, like a slipping banana,
Gravity's pranksters, they play the bandana.
As we orbit along in a giggly trance,
The universe twirls in a whimsical dance!

Threads of the Celestial Tapestry

In the cosmic loom, where threads intertwine,
Space yarns stories, both silly and fine.
Galaxies weave jokes with colorful threads,
Creating a tapestry where laughter spreads!

Supernova sequins shine bright with delight,
While shooting stars flash their jokes in the night.
A satellite spins with a wink and a twirl,
Broadcasting giggles across the wide world!

Constellations pose, like stars on the stage,
Playing roles that seem quite out of gauge.
Orion spills coffee, as he leads the parade,
While Cassiopeia's antics never do fade!

Together they laugh, in orchestrated schemes,
Tickling the cosmos with whimsical dreams.
Each thread a delight, in this vast cosmic tale,
Where humor's the ship that forever will sail!

Dances with Distant Suns

Suns waltz through space, with a twinkle and flair,
Throwing cosmic parties, without a care.
Planets join in, in a galactic ballet,
As moons do the cha-cha, while laughing away!

Rings of Saturn spin in a haphazard way,
Shooting joy into orbits that happily sway.
Stars prance along, with a sparkle and gleam,
Creating a show, beyond any dream!

Distant galaxies join in the fun,
With gravitational pulls that weigh a ton.
But laughter's their gravity, keeping them close,
In this dance of creation, they surely boast!

In the void of space, where silence once ruled,
Now echoes of laughter are joyfully pooled.
A universe shimmering, with smiles that hum,
In the dance of the cosmos, we all come undone!

Veins of the Universe

Stars are winking with a grin,
While planets spin in a dizzy din.
Galaxies twist like a cosmic dance,
Just don't let black holes take your chance.

Asteroids are like dodging flies,
The spacecraft's got some wild ties.
Shooting comets zip and zoom,
Check your helmet, beware the boom!

Little aliens laugh at Earth,
They wonder what our laughter's worth.
On Tuesday, they play hide and seek,
In a nebula, so mystique.

And if they invite us over for tea,
Let's not forget the gravity!
We'll float and giggle in zero-G,
Just as long as no one has to pee!

Harmony in Distant Rhythms

A planet sings a high-pitched tune,
While moons dance under a silvery moon.
Nebulas swirl in vibrant hues,
Kind of like paint on a cosmic muse.

Space whales glide with graceful flair,
Bubbling joys in the brisk cold air.
They serenade with a deep bass hum,
And make constellations out of fun!

Astro-dogs chase their tails at night,
While cats just float, looking for a bite.
In this vastness, silly dreams arise,
As laughter echoes through the skies!

We'll dance upon the rings of Saturn,
In a cosmic party that's never pattern.
Hold on tight, for this ride is wild,
In the harmony of space, we'll be the child!

Lullabies of the Milky Way

Close your eyes, drift into space,
The stars are keeping a smiling face.
Whispers of asteroids gently hum,
A lullaby from the cosmic drum.

Shooting stars play peek-a-boo,
They wink at you and wish come true.
Stardust hugs from a galaxy bright,
Sending dreams into the night.

Space kitties nap on soft, cloud beds,
While comet tails dance over their heads.
Expecting treats from a far-off sun,
In this universe, there's always fun!

So let the cosmos rock you slow,
As the Milky Way puts on a show.
With every twinkle, a cozy cheer,
Goodnight, sweet traveler, never fear!

The Chronicles of Lightyears

Flip through pages of starlit lore,
With tales of planets and so much more.
Chronicles spun in a cosmic web,
From supernovas to a silly ebb.

Distant worlds with oddball quirks,
Where rubber ducks and jelly lurks.
Alien parties throw confetti wide,
As interstellar blush cats take pride.

Time travelers show up for dinner,
With sandwiches that are a real winner.
Keep your secrets locked up tight,
For they may steal a bite at night!

So buckle up for this intergalactic ride,
With laughter lighting up the tide.
For every lightyear we boldly fly,
Adds a chuckle to the cosmic pie!

Starlight Serenades of the Unknown

In the depths of space, I lost my cat,
Searching high and low, should've brought a hat.
He's riding comets, that little brat,
Eating stardust, how 'bout that?

Aliens giggle, they think it's grand,
My feline's fame spreads through the land.
He's a space hero, isn't that planned?
With a fish-shaped ship, he'll take a stand!

Whispers of laughter drift through the stars,
As he dances with asteroids and pink candy bars.
Purring in zero-G, oh what bizarre!
Come join the fun, let's raise our jars!

So if you see him, give a loud shout,
He's the kitty with swagger, no doubt about.
In the cosmos, he's king, without a pout,
I'm just the human, trying to figure it out.

Echoing Sounds of a Hidden Galaxy

In a galaxy far, where chaos reigns,
A cow moos loudly, it's driving me insane.
Playing cosmic tunes, on galactic trains,
While planets spin slow, like tired old chains.

Strange echoes bounce, like a cosmic game,
A chicken walks by, wearing a name.
Laughter erupts, isn't it all the same?
We all know space is a little bit lame.

Squirrels in space suits, making a toast,
To flying spaghetti, we gather and boast.
With meatball meteors, we've earned the most,
In this wacky world, we're never engrossed.

So here's to the sounds, from afar they play,
A medley of nonsense, brightens my day.
With raucous laughter, we'll dance and sway,
In this hidden galaxy, we'll forever stay.

The Brightness Between Us

In a twinkle of starlight, we share our dreams,
Floating through space, or so it seems.
You pass me a donut, with glowing creams,
We chuckle in zero-G, bursting at the seams.

Your smile shines brighter than a quasar's light,
We play tag with planets, what a silly sight!
In cosmic warm hugs, everything feels right,
As we twirl through the void, like stars in flight.

Galactic giggles, we dance up high,
With asteroid confetti, just my you and I.
We toast with stardust, as cosmic pies fly,
Drifting through laughter, our spirits comply.

So let's paint the heavens with colors so bold,
In our brilliant friendship, a treasure to hold.
Amidst all the wonders, more precious than gold,
The brightness between us will never grow old.

Twilight in the Intergalactic Void

The twilight creeps in, with a wink and a grin,
A space raccoon steals my dinner again.
He juggles my fries, oh, where have you been?
This galactic buffet is full of chagrin.

Invisible bunnies hop through the dark,
Wearing tiny spacesuits, making their mark.
They sing silly songs, oh what a lark!
As stars twinkle down, sparking a spark.

With nebulas swirling, and moons giving chase,
A penguin appears, in a tutu, a race!
He slips on space ice, oh what a disgrace,
As I laugh uncontrollably, the void's warm embrace.

So gather your friends, in this odd cosmic dance,
Where twilight births laughter, it's all just chance.
In the intergalactic void, take a glance,
At the whimsy of life, grabbing every chance.

www.ingramcontent.com/pod-product-compliance
Lightning Source LLC
Chambersburg PA
CBHW071835160426
43209CB00003B/311